Lunar Mysteries Co

Written and Illustrated
by
Heather Valentin

For Lacy Sunshine

©Heather Valentin. Lacy Sunshine. All rights reserved.
Personal use only. No redistribution without artist's consent.
Absolutely no sharing, pposting uncolored black and white line art
anywhere on social media etc. without written permisson from the artist.

Sneak Peek of my new soon to be released coloring book titled

"Li'l Bellyfulls"

for Lay Sunshine.

Enjoy,....

Bunny Trio Bellyfulls

Unicorn Bellyfulls

and Yummy Hunny Bellyfulls.

Hugs,
Heather

www.lacysunshine.weebly.com

Sneak peek for you of my new upcoming
soon to be released coloring book
titled

"Romantiques"

For Lacy Sunshine.

Enjoy...
April Showers Romantique.

Hugs,
Heather

Made in the USA
Lexington, KY
23 July 2018